WOMEN IN THE BOOK OF MORMON
STUDY GUIDE

BY
HEATHER FARRELL

WOMEN IN THE SCRIPTURES
WWW.WOMENINTHESCRIPTURES.COM

ALMA 32:23

And now, he imparteth his word by angels
unto men, yea, not only men but women also.
Now this is not all; little children do have
words given unto them many times, which
confound the wise and the learned.

INTRODUCTION

I'm excited that you have picked up this study guide and that you are undertaking a personal study of the women in The Book of Mormon. People often assume that there are not very many women in The Book of Mormon, but I hope that you can tell from the size of this Study Guide that such an assumption is not true. While there aren't many women mentioned by name, only five—Eve, Sarah, Sariah, Abish and Isabel—there are more than 80 references to unnamed women, and dozens more scriptures including teachings addressed to women or about women.

This study guide is designed to help you slow down and discover women in The Book of Mormon that you didn't even didn't even know were there. They have incredible stories and many of them have important lessons for our day. Don't let their lack of names make them any less real to you. These were real women, who lived, breathed and struggled with many of the same problems women of today. I hope that as you study these women you will become familiar with their stories and feel confident giving them names and sharing their stories, with your family, friends or in church.

I hope that the resources and questions I have included will help you take your study of these Book of Mormon women to a deeper level. I hope you will gain a love for them and gain a testimony that women have essential roles and parts to play in God's work. Mostly, I hope that as you study you will deepen your love for Jesus Christ and learn what he would have you do to spread His love and His work.

Happy Scripture Studying!

HOW TO USE THIS STUDY GUIDE

Step 1 -- Print off and organize your Study Guide.

If you have the PDF version of this Study Guide you will want to first print it off and then either have it spiral bound or three-hole-punch it and put it in a binder. Either way is fine. If you have the bound copy of this study guide then you are good to go. Before you begin your study you may want to make photocopies of some of the additional pages found in the back of the Study Guide. These additional pages are intended to help you take your study of the women in The Book of Mormon a bit deeper, they include things like character study, timeline, and compare and contrast sheets. Having them printed off before you begin your study will make it easier to use them when you decide you'd like to study a woman or a topic more in-depth. Then when you are finished with your study you can paste these additional pages into your study guide so that you can keep all your notes together.

Step 2—Open up the Book of Mormon and start reading.

Please note that I have only included real women, those who lived and breathed during Book of Mormon times, in this study guide. I also only included women who are unique to the Book of Mormon. This means while several other Old and New Testament women are mentioned (like Eve and Sarah) you will not find pages for them. There are blank study pages in the back of the Study Guide for any additional women you'd like to study.

Before you begin you may also want to make a list of questions that you would like to have answered through your study of the women in the Book of Mormon. Write them in the front and then look for answers as you study. I think you will be surprised what the Holy Ghost will teach you as you diligently study the scriptures.

Step 3—Go slow and take time to ponder.

When I study my scriptures I take time to stop on each woman and ask myself several questions to help me ponder on her and her story. These questions may be helpful to you in your study as well.

What is unique about this woman and her story?

How does she fit into the time period in which she lived?

What Christ-like qualities does she exemplify?

What would I ask her if I could meet her?

How can I relate to her?

What can I (or someone else I know) learn from her experiences?

Remember don't worry about how long your study takes you. The point is not to see how fast you can run through the Book of Mormon but how deep into it you can go. Give yourself permission to slow down and take as much time as you need or want to study each woman and each story. You may also want to mark or highlight in your scriptures all the references to women and women's stories so that you can find them again easily.

Step 4—Share what you learn.

An important part of scripture study is learning to "reflect" or organize what you have learned. As you study find a way in which you can share what you are learning about these women with someone else. This may be as simple as just talking to a family member or friend about it or you may want to write, draw or doodle something in your journal or study guide that summarizes what you have learned. In addition, I hope that your study of these women will inspire you to share their stories confidently in church settings, like Sunday School, Relief Society, Priesthood quorums, Young Women's and Young Men's and in Sacrament meeting. The more that we can use their names and share the stories the more these women will emerge from the pages of the scriptures and come into the light, where they belong.

ADDITIONAL RESOURCES TO USE

You will find that studying the women of The Book of Mormon is different than studying the women of the Old and New Testaments. This is mainly because we do not have many resources, outside of The Book of Mormon, for studying things like the geography, history, culture, etc. of Book of Mormon peoples. We also don't have any other translations or historical documents to compare the text to like we do the Old and New Testaments. At first this lack of outside documents or resources may seem like a hindrance to an in-depth study of these women, but I think you will find that if you invite Him into your study the Holy Ghost will be able to teach you everything you need to know. You may not figure out exactly where the "narrow neck of land" is, but you probably will be taught the powerful spiritual principles and doctrines these women's stories teach.

I have tried to include resources and questions in my "Ideas for Additional Study" sections that can help guide and inspire your scripture study. In addition to these resources you may also want to use:

1826 Webster's Dictionary

This is one the oldest English dictionaries and it is a valuable resource in your study. Even though The Book of Mormon was translated into English less than 200 years ago many meanings and usages of words have changed. It can be helpful to look up words in this dictionary in order to know what the older meaning (the one Joseph Smith would have intended) of a word would have been. When you do look up words make sure to write them down in your study guide under the "Words I looked up" section or to write the meanings in your scriptures. You can find this dictionary online or in print form.

Online Scriptures

The Church of Jesus Christ of Latter-day Saints has a wonderful online search tool for the scriptures that can be found at scriptures.LDS.org. Several times in this Study Guide I will encourage you to look up words or phrases on this website using the "search" bar on the right side. The online scriptures can be a fast and easy way to find ways in which a word, or similar phrase, is used elsewhere in the scriptures. It can also help you connect scriptures together in ways that you might not have thought of before. It can also just be a fast way to find a scripture that you can't remember the reference for!

Index of The Book of Mormon

The index, found at the end of the triple combination (The Book of Mormon, The Doctrine and Covenants and The Pearl of Great Price) is a great resource for studying The Book of Mormon. Not only does it list many of the names and places in The Book of Mormon and all the scriptures where they are mentioned, but it also gives you lists of scriptures that are specific to the triple combination. I don't always advocate for ignoring the scriptures listed in the Old and New Testaments, but there may be times when it is helpful to study a topic or a doctrine with just the scriptures listed in the Index.

Pronouncing Guide

At the very end of The Book of Mormon there is a Pronouncing Guide which can be helpful in learning how to correctly say the names of The Book of Mormon. For example sometimes people say the name "Abish" with as short "a" as in "map" or "ask" when it should be pronounced with a long "a" as in "able". If you are ever unsure about how to pronounce a name or a place make sure to look it up. If you are interested in knowing more about where the Pronouncing Guide came from there is a good Ensign article in the July 1996 edition by Donald W. Parry entitled, "I Have a Question."

RESOURCES IN THE APPENDIX

You will also find several resources in the appendix of this Study Guide that will help you with your study as well. They include:

Character Sketch

Use this page to study a character from the scriptures more in-depth. Write their name (or a draw a picture) in the center square and then make a list or a "cloud" of all the attributes, virtues and character traits you see in them as you study. This page can also be used to do a topical study on a word, like "faith" or "virtue".

Timeline

Use this page to create timelines of events in The Book of Mormon. Don't be too concerned with getting dates right, you just want to get an idea of what events happened in order. You may need to tape several of them together for some of the longer histories and chapters in The Book of Mormon.

Storyboard

Use this page to draw (or write) out a story from The Book of Mormon. This can be a visual way to keep track of people, places and events. Don't stress out if you are a good artist, this is just to help you keep track of the story and notice details you may have missed.

Compare and Contrast

There are several different compare and contrast sheets. Choose which one to use depending on how many different stories or characters you are comparing and contrasting. For example, you may want to use these pages to compare the differences between two groups of people, like the Lamanites or Nephites or between individuals like the Daughter of Jared and the Daughter(s) of Omer.

Pride Cycle Sheet

The Book of Mormon is full of Pride Cycles, both in individuals and nations, use this sheet to document the pride cycles you notice as you study. You may want to do several throughout your study of The Book of Mormon and then compare what is similar and different between them.

Scatter Chart

This page is a brainstorming page to help you organize and record thoughts you have about a certain topic or person. Begin by writing the topic, story or person you are studying in the center circle and then draw smaller circles coming off of the bigger circle with thoughts and ideas you have as you study. The idea of this type of study is to help you make lists of ideas, principles or concepts that you can link together and see patterns in.

Scripture references:

1 Nephi 2:5
1 Nephi 5:1-9
1 Nephi 8:14
1 Nephi 17:55
1 Nephi 18:17-19
1 Nephi 18:7
(Jacob & Joseph born)

What I know about her:

Words I looked up:

Questions I have about her:

MY THOUGHTS:

Additional scriptures I studied:

Ideas for additional study:

Do a character sketch for Sariah. What are her strengths and what are her weaknesses? How does she turn weaknesses to strengths?

Though she is not mentioned by name, 1 Nephi 1:1 states that Nephi was born of "goodly parents." As you study Nephi 1 pay special attention to what type of family and upbringing he had. What can you learn about Sariah from his descriptions? Also, look up the word "goodly" in the 1828 Webster's dictionary to better understand what the word means.

Lehi and Sariah were contemporaries of the prophet Jeremiah and lived in Jerusalem about 600 BC under the reign of King Zedekiah. Not long after they left Jerusalem was conquered by Babylon and the Jews were taken captive. To better understand their situation study 2 Kings 23- 25, 2 Chronicles 35-36. and "Zedekiah" in the Bible Dictionary (page ~~792~~ 745). The book of Jeremiah also goes into great-er detail about this time period and the destruction of Jerusalem. *Also Lamentations of Jeremiah* 52

Sariah gives birth to two children during her journey in the wilderness. How old do you imagine her to be? What types of additional struggles would she have faced as a (twice) pregnant and breastfeeding mother? How might you (or somone you know) relate to her?

FIVE DAUGHTERS OF ISHMAEL

Scripture references:

1 Nephi 7: 1, 6-8, 19
1 Nephi 16: 7, 27,
35-36
1 Nephi 18:9
Alma 3:7

What I know about them:

Words I looked up:

Questions I have about them:

MY THOUGHTS:

Additional scriptures I studied:

Ideas for additional study:

For this page draw five women (don't worry, they can be stick figures) and number them 1-5. As you study these women write down attributes or characteristics of the different daughters. Even though we don't know their names we can get a feel for how different they each were and what types of choices they made.

We know that there were four brothers-- Laman, Lemuel, Sam and Nephi-- and that they each married one of the daughters of Ishmael. The eldest daughter of Ishmael married Laban's servant Zoram. Based off what you have read about the different temperaments and actions of Ishmael's daughters make a guess at which ones married which men. Draw corresponding men for your drawings of the five daughters, with who you think would have been a good match for each man.

How is the murmuring that Ishmael's daughters did in 1 Nephi 16:35-36 similar to the murmuring Sariah did in 1 Nephi 5: 1-9? How do you think you would have responded in a similar circumstance? What can their experience teach us about murmuring and how to handle challenges in our lives?

HMAEL'S WIFE

Scripture references:

1 Nephi 7: 6, 19

What I know about her:

Words I looked up:

Questions I have about her:

MY THOUGHTS:

Additional scriptures I studied:

Ideas for additional study:

Do a character sketch for her. What type of family challenges do you think she would have faced? How is she similar to Sariah? How is she different?

In 1 Nephi 7:5 it says that "the Lord did soften the heart of Ishmael, and also his household, insomuch that they took their journey with us down into the wilderness." Why type of experiences do you think she had that gave her the courage to leave? When have you made a choice similar to hers?

While making the trip from Jerusalem to where Lehi's family was in the wilderness Laman and Lemuel, as well as most of the family of Ishmael rebelled against Nephi and wanted to return to Jerusalem. When an attempt was made on Nephi's life Ishmael's wife was among the few who spoke up for him and defended him. What do her actions in the wilderness tell you about what type of woman she was? How do you think she felt to have her family divided? Does she remind you of any women you know?

NEPHI'S WIFE

Scripture references:

1 Nephi 16:7
1 Nephi 18:19

What I know about her:

Words I looked up:

Questions I have about her:

MY THOUGHTS:

Additional scriptures I studied:

Ideas for additional study:

Look back at the pictures you drew of Ishmael's five daughters. Which one of them do you think Nephi married? Why did you choose her?

What qualities did she have that made her a good wife for Nephi? What do you think he saw in her that led him to love her? How did she help him in fulfill his calling from the Lord? How might you use her story to help young women prepare for marriage?

As you study 1 Nephi make a list of all the challenges and persecutions that Nephi faces. How do you think these events affected her and her children? How does she respond to these challenges?

Just like Emma Smith, the wife of Joseph Smith, Nephi's wife was also the wife of a young prophet who faced persecution. Their situations are similar in many ways. Using what you know of Emma Smith's life do a compare and contrast study between her and Nephi's wife. How are they similar? How are they different?

Scripture references:

1 Nephi 17:1-2, 20
1 Nephi 18: 6
2 Nephi 5:6

What I know about them:

Words I looked up:

Questions I have about them:

MY THOUGHTS:

Additional scriptures I studied:

Ideas for additional study:

Make a list of all the things that the women who traveled with Lehi's family faced. What extra challenges did they face because they were women? Do you think you would have been able to endure what they had to in the wilderness? Would you have murmured?

We don't know how many women actually traveled with Lehi's family. It might help to draw a picture or make a list of all the women you know were included, remembering that there were probably others who aren't mentioned.

What do you think it means when Nephi says that the women "were strong, yeah, even like unto the men." (1 Nephi 17:2) Why do you think he includes so much about what they went through?

Why do you think Nephi doesn't mention that he has sisters earlier on in his account? Do you think he is referring to biological sisters? If not, what other type of "sisters" could they be? What significant choices do they make?

DAUGHTERS OF LAMAN AND LEMUEL

Scripture references:

2 Nephi 4: 3-9

What I know about them:

Words I looked up:

Questions I have about them:

MY THOUGHTS:

Additional scriptures I studied:

Ideas for additional study:

Make a list of the things that Lehi promises the posterity of Laman and Lemuel in his blessing (2 Nephi 4:3-9). How do you see these promises fulfilled later on in the Book of Mormon?

In verse 6 Lehi talks about a "curse", what do you think this means? It may be helpful to study the word "curse" in the Index of the Triple Combination (page 69). What can you discover about how God uses the word "cursed"? What does someone have to do to become cursed, and how is it manifest? You might even consider writing your own definition of what this word means after you finish your study.

Do a compare and contrast between the counsel Lehi gives to to Laman and Lemuel's families and the counsel he gives Jacob (2 Nephi 2) and Joseph (2 Nephi 3)? What is similar? What is different? What happens to each of these groups after Lehi's death (see 2 Nephi 5)?

Imagine that you were on your deathbed, like Lehi was. What counsel you would want to give your family before you died? Take time to write down your ideas. You may even want to consider writing a letter to put in your journal, your will, or another special place.

NDER, CHASTE AND DELICATE NEPHITE WOMEN

Scripture references:

Jacob 2:7-9, 31-33, 35

What I know about them:

Words I looked up:

Questions I have about them:

MY THOUGHTS:

Additional scriptures I studied:

Ideas for additional study:

In Jacob 2: 7 Jacob uses the words tender, chaste and delicate to describe these women and says that it "is pleasing unto God." What do these words mean to you and why do you think these are attributes that are pleasing unto God? How can you develop these attributes or help the young women in your life develop them?

Jacob gives some interesting insight into the Lord's law of marriage and plural marriage in Jacob 2: 23- 35. Study these verses closely making note of what the Lord's law is concerning marriage (Jacob 2:27) and when He makes exceptions to that law (Jacob 2:30). Underline or make a list of the reason why the Lord did not approve of plural marriage among the Nephites, and how the women were affected by the men taking more wives and concubines. What do you think are God's reasons for allowing plural marriage in some cases and forbidding it in others?

Can you relate to these Nephite women whose "sobbings of their hearts ascend up to God" (Jacob 2:35) and whose prayers the Lord heard and answered? When has God heard the sobbings of your heart and how has He answered your prayers? Take time to record an experience in your study guide or journal.

WIVES OF THE LAMANITES

Scripture references:

Jacob 3:5-7

What I know about them:

Words I looked up:

Questions I have about them:

MY THOUGHTS:

Additional scriptures I studied:

Ideas for additional study:

What is the commandment that the Lamanites had not forgotten to keep? What does the Lord promise would happen to them because they had not forgotten this commandment? How do you see this promise fulfilled throughout the Book of Mormon?

Compare and contrast the differences between the Lamanite women mentioned here and the Nephite women mentioned in Jacob 2. What is similar about them and what is different? What types of challenges and blessings would each group face? If you had to choose to be among one group, which would you choose? Why?

How do Jacob's words about marriage and family still apply to our world today? How might you use these scriptures to teach about God's law of marriage to your family or in your church calling?

OMEN WHO ATTENDED KING BENJAMIN'S SPEECH

Scripture references:

Mosiah 2:5
Mosiah 4: 1-3
Mosiah 5:2-5, 7
Mosiah 6:1-2

What I know about them:

Words I looked up:

Questions I have about them:

MY THOUGHTS:

Additional scriptures I studied:

Ideas for additional study:

Make a timeline of the Nephite leaders starting with Nephi and ending with King Benjamin by quickly scanning through 1 Nephi- Mosiah. You may want to underline each of the leaders you find in Omni . Make note of how much time has passed and what major events transpired in between.

Draw a picture of what the temple grounds must have looked like in preparation for King Benjamin's address. How would families have been situated? How many people do you think were present? What types of challenges might such a large gathering of people presented? What do you think it would have been like to be there?

Study King Benjamin's address (Mosiah 2- Mosiah 5) making note of his main points and how the multitude (women included) reacted to his words. Have you ever had a spiritual experience similar to the one these women had? If not, what do you need to do to have one?

In Mosiah 5:7 King Benjamin says that those who have covenanted with Christ have been "spiritually begotten" by him. Take the time to study the scripture references in the footnotes for verse 7, pondering on why the image of birth is one that is used often used to describe Christ's relationship with us and how that might have special meaning for women.

WIVES OF THE MEN WHO WENT TO FIND THE LAND OF NEPHI

Scripture references:

Mosiah 9:2

What I know about them:

Words I looked up:

Questions I have about them:

MY THOUGHTS:

Additional scriptures I studied:

Ideas for additional study:

Omni 1:27- 29 gives the back story to Zeniff's record. Study these verses in addition to Mosiah 9: 1-2 to get a good picture of what the situation was and who Zeniff was. It might help to write the words "who, what, when, where, how" and fill in the answers as you study.

At this point in the Book of Mormon it can get hard to keep track of all the different groups of people. It may be helpful to make a timeline or a rough map (don't worry about geogrpahy, just keeping track of where each group is and where they go) for Mosiah 9-22 highlighting the main events and the different groups that break off or come together.

OMEN OF THE PEOPLE OF ZENIFF

Scripture references:

Mosiah 10:5, 9

What I know about them:

Words I looked up:

Questions I have about them:

MY THOUGHTS:

Additional scriptures I studied:

Ideas for additional study:

Though they aren't specifically mentioned, women were included from the start of Zeniff's journey, which begins in Mosiah 9: 3. As you study his account pay attention to what the women would have experienced and how you think they might have been involved.

What do you think would have motivated women to go with Zeniff and search for the land of Nephi? How can you relate to them? What types of things do you seek and yearn after?

It is interesting to note that in the first attempt to find the land of Nephi (Mosiah 9: 1-2, Omni 1:27-29) that it doesn't mention any women being included in the group. Do you think the lack of women may have contributed to the first group's failure? Why or why not?

WIVES & CONCUBINES OF KING NOAH & HIS WICKED PRIESTS

Scripture references:

Mosiah 11:2, 4, 14
Mosiah 20:3

What I know about them:

Words I looked up:

Questions I have about them:

MY THOUGHTS:

Additional scriptures I studied:

Ideas for additional study:

Study Abinadi's sermon (Mosiah 11: 20- 16: 15) making a list of his main points. Then imagine that you were one of these wives or concubines listening to his words. What do you think would stand out to you? Would you have been happy with his words or upset?

How would life have been different for these women after Noah was killed and the wicked priests ran away into the wilderness? What do you think happened to them? Do you think any of them may have joined Alma's group? Why or why not?

Scripture references:

Mosiah 19:9 -24; 20:11

What I know about them:

Words I looked up:

Questions I have about them:

MY THOUGHTS:

Additional scriptures I studied:

Ideas for additional study:

What roles do women play as peacemakers in the Book of Mormon? Make a list of the ones you find as you study the Book of Mormon. How is the role of a peacemaker an influential one for women in the Book of Mormon and how might this be an important message for modern day women to consider as they study it?

How were the "fair daughters" of the people of Noah peacemakers? In what ways did they show bravery and charity? How could their example be used to teach the young women in your life?

What other examples can you think of in the scriptures where a beautiful woman was able to prevent war, violence, or save her people? Do you think that these women were successful because they were beautiful or did they possess other attributes that made them powerful peacemakers?

How do you think you would have felt if you were one of the women whose husband fled into the wilderness without you? How would you feel when he returned? How do you think this experience could have either strengthened or weakened a family?

24 DAUGHTERS OF THE LAMANITES

Scripture references:

Mosiah 20:1-23
Mosiah 21: 20-21
Mosiah 23:33-34
Mosiah 25:12

What I know about them:

Words I looked up:

Questions I have about them:

MY THOUGHTS:

Additional scriptures I studied:

Ideas for additional study:

The footnote in Mosiah 20:1 links to a story in Judges 21:21. Do you think that the wicked priests may have been familiar with this story? What similarities do you see between these two stories and these two groups of women?

How would this story have been different if the Lamanties had communicated first instead of attacked? What can this story teach you about not reacting to situations with anger and judgement? How can that lesson be applied in your life?

Make a timeline of the experiences of the wicked priests (also called the people of Amulon) paying special attention to how much time passes in between events and what these women would have experienced. Their story begins in Mosiah 19.

Why do you think that these women did not accept their freedom when it was offered them? Why do you think they choose to protect their captors (ie. husbands)? What lesson do you think can be learned from them?

Scripture references:

Mosiah 21:9-11-17
Mosiah 22:2, 8

What I know about them:

Words I looked up:

Questions I have about them:

MY THOUGHTS:

Additional scriptures I studied:

Ideas for additional study:

D&C 83 describes the ideal way in which widows and fatherless children should be cared for. Study D&C 83 and outline what the Lord teaches. Do the people Limhi live up to the Lord's expectations of caring for widows? Why or why not?

How would your community be changed if the majority of women became widows? What roles do you think women would choose, or be compelled, to assume? What benefits and challenges would there be?

Compare and contrast the story of the people of Limhi (Mosiah 21 and 22) with the story of the people of Alma (Mosiah 23 and 24). Both groups of people escape captivity, and do so in very similar ways, but there are some key differences. What do you think is significant about their different approaches and what can you learn from their different ways of responding to the same challenge?

WOMEN WHO JOINED THE PEOPLE OF ALMA

Scripture references:

Mosiah 23:28
Mosiah 24:22

What I know about them:

Words I looked up:

Questions I have about them:

MY THOUGHTS:

Additional scriptures I studied:

Ideas for additional study:

The women who went with Alma were those who heard him preach at the Waters of Mormon (Mosiah 18). Go back and study all of Mosiah 18. Make a list of what these women would have been taught and what promises they would have made. What did these women risk in order to be baptized and to believe Alma's teachings? What can you learn from their conversion story?

What is your coversion story? Even if you were born a member of the Chruch you still have one. Take time to write it down either in this study guide or in your journal.

How does prayer and faith factor into these women's experiences? What can you learn about prayer from them?

What happens to these women after their escape from the Lamanites (see Mosiah 23-24)? Draw a story board of their experiences. As you study the rest of the book of Mosiah keep these women, and the women of the people of Limhi in mind, remembering that they are often in the background of the story.

OMEN OF THE PEOPLE OF MINON AND NEPHI

Scripture references:

Alma 2:25- 26
Alma 3:1-2

What I know about them:

Words I looked up:

Questions I have about them:

MY THOUGHTS:

Additional scriptures I studied:

Ideas for additional study:

The conflict in Alma 2 is initiated by a man named Amlici who followed the teachings of Nehor (Alma 1). Study Alma 1 by highlighting or listing the things that Nehor taught and what effect his teaching had on the people. What examples do we see today of "Nehor-ish" teachings? How can modern day followers of Christ be deceived by similar teachings today?

Draw, or imagine, a picture of what these women would have experienced. How is war different for women and children? What additional hardships do women face in conflict? Why would the Amlicities have killed women and children?

It is important to remember that throughout history women have often traveled with military campaigns, usually as cooks, laundresses, or as companions. It is very likely that women also traveled with the Nephite and Lamantie armies. How does this knowledge help you "see" the unmentioned women in the conflicts between the Nephites and the Lamanties?

WOMEN OF GIDEON

Scripture references:

Alma 7:27

What I know about them:

Words I looked up:

Questions I have about them:

MY THOUGHTS:

Additional scriptures I studied:

Ideas for additional study:

Previous to his visit to Gideon Alma preached in Zarahemla. Study Alma 5 and 6 to see what he taught them and why. What sort of things were the people struggling with?

How are the people of Gideon different from the people of Zarahemla? What is different about the way in which Alma teaches the people of Gideon versus how he teaches the people of Zarahemla? What does this tell you about the type of women who were among his audience?

Mary, the Mother of Christ is spoken of in Alma 7:10 and she is also mentioned by name in Mosiah 3:8. She is the only woman in scripture whose name was known before her birth. Why do you think it was important for the Nephites to know her name? If you would like to do a deeper study on Mary in the Book of Mormon the scriptures refering to her are 1 Nephi 11:12-21; 2 Nephi: 17:14; Mosiah 3: 8-10 and Alma 7:10.

Scripture references:

Alma 10:11

What I know about them:

Words I looked up:

Questions I have about them:

MY THOUGHTS:

Additional scriptures I studied:

Ideas for additional study:

Amulek told the people that Alma had "blessed mine house" (Alma 10:11) including the women who lived with him. Study Alma 8: 18-27 which tells about the meeting between Alma and Amulek. What role do you think the women played in welcoming Alma and ministering to his physical needs? What type of blessings do you think they received? How can you relate to these women?

In Alma 10: 1-10 Amulek tells us about himself and his family. What can learn about Amulek from these verses? What can you learn about the women (like his wife and daughters) who would have lived with Amulek? How would their lives have changed after meeting Alma?

Some of the most vocal opponents of Amulek (and his household) were the judges and lawyers, including a man named Zeezrom. Study Alma 10 and 11 highlighting, or making a list, of Zeezrom's main arguments and interests. How are these same arguments still being used today? In addition highlight or make a list of how Amulek refutes these arguments. How can you follow his example when dealing with people like Zeezrom?

WOMEN AND CHILDREN BURNED FOR THEIR BELIEF IN GOD

Scripture references:

Alma 14:8-11, 14
Alma 15:2

What I know about them:

Words I looked up:

Questions I have about them:

MY THOUGHTS:

Additional scriptures I studied:

Ideas for additional study:

What happened to many of the husbands and fathers of these women and children (see Alma 14: 7 and 15:1)? Do you think that Amulek's own wife and children may have been among them?

What does it mean to be a martyr? Look up "martyr" it up in the 1828 Webster's dictionary and in the Bible Dictionary. Make a list of people from the scriptures and church history who are considered to be martyrs. Would you consider these women and children to be martyrs? Why or why not?

Pretend like you are writing a letter to a friend who is struggling with why God allows bad things to happen to good people and innocent children. Study Alma 14: 10-11 and Alma 60:12-13 and then write out what you would say to your friend. Be sure to include scriptures and examples supporting your ideas in your response.

AUGHTERS OF KING LAMONI

Scripture references:

Alma 17:24
Alma 18:43

What I know about them:

Words I looked up:

Questions I have about them:

MY THOUGHTS:

Additional scriptures I studied:

Ideas for additional study:

These daughters are only mentioned twice, both times in the context of their father King Lamoni. How do you think their lives changed after their father's conversion? How has your life been influenced by the conversion stories of your family or ancestors? Or if you are a convert, how do you think your conversion story will influence future generations?

What does it take to make a strong convert? So often people join the church, only to fall away from it shortly after. What do you think makes some people strong in the gosepl and others not?

King Lamoni's people eventually become the Anti-Nephi-Lehis (see Alma 23-27) and these daughters would have been included in that group. Make a timeline of the events surrounding this group of people (Alma 17- 27). What types of experiences would these young women have had? How can their example be used to teach the young women in your life?

WIFE OF KING LAMONI

Scripture references:

Alma 18:43
Alma 19:2-3, 17-18,
28-30

What I know about her:

Words I looked up:

Questions I have about her:

MY THOUGHTS:

Additional scriptures I studied:

Ideas for additional study:

Do a character sketch for her. She exhibits some powerful gifts of the spirit. Make a list of which gifts she possess and how she uses them (for a list of gifts of the spirit see D&C 46:11-25). What impresses you most about her?

Use her story to do a study on faith. Study the definition of "faith" given in the Bible Dictionary (page 669) and write down phrases that you think describe King Lamoni's wife. What can she teach you about faith? What role did her faith play in King Lamoni's conversion and in the conversion of her people?

She is one of the few women in the Book of Mormon whose actual words are recorded. In fact the only other woman who is quoted in the Book of Mormon is Sariah and it is only one line. Yet in Alma 19 we have several long quotes of this Queen's words. You may want to mark them in your scriptures. Who do you think took the time to write them down and why would they have been preserved?

Scripture references:

Alma 19:16-17, 28-29

What I know about her:

Words I looked up:

Questions I have about her:

MY THOUGHTS:

Additional scriptures I studied:

Ideas for additional study:

Do a character sketch for her. What do you know about her history? About her faith? About the desires of her heart? How did the Lord make the desires of her heart happen?

What can Abish teach you about missionary work? Make a list of all the things she did before she gained success as a missionary. How can you follow her example?

Abish was converted to the Lord through a spiritual experience her father had. What do you imagine this experienced entailed? What can her story teach about the importance of father-daughter relationships?

In Alma 47:23 there is an interesting scripture about raising people up from the ground. How might this scripture apply (or not apply) to the story of Abish, Ammon, and King Lamoni and his wife? What significance do you see in all the falling-to-the-earth-and-being-raised-up-again action in this story?

QUEEN OF THE LAMANTIES (MOTHER OF KING LAMONI)

Scripture references:

Alma 22:19-24

What I know about her:

Words I looked up:

Questions I have about her:

MY THOUGHTS:

Additional scriptures I studied:

Ideas for additional study:

Do a character sketch for her. What are her strengths? What are her weaknesses? Who does she remind you of?

Do a compare and contrast sheet for her story and the story of King Lamoni's wife (Alma 18:43; 19: 2-3, 17-18, 28-30). What is similar about their stories? Why are their experiences so different?

These Lamanities witnessed many miracles. How do you think these miracles contributed to their conversion process? Which comes first the miracle or the faith? Do a topic study on miracles by studying the scriptures listed under "Miracle" in the Index of your Triple Combination. Take time to write about when you have witnessed a miracle.

IDOWS OF THE MEN SLAIN PROTECTING THE PEOPLE OF AMMON

Scripture references:

Alma 28:5, 12

What I know about them:

Words I looked up:

Questions I have about them:

MY THOUGHTS:

Additional scriptures I studied:

Ideas for additional study:

How did these women react to their loss (see Alma 28:6, 11-12)? What can their attitudes teach you about how to respond to tragedy and loss in your own life?

It is important to remember that before their conversion the people of Ammon (also called the Anti-Nephi-Lehi's) were Lamanties and the enemies of the Nephites. Study the history of the people of Ammon (Alma 24-27) and think about what type of love and forgiveness it would have taken for the Nephites to have given them a portion of their land and to have used their armies (at great cost) to defend them. How would you feel if you were in these women's shoes?

WOMEN LED ASTRAY BY KORIHOR

Scripture references:

Alma 30:18

What I know about them:

Words I looked up:

Questions I have about them:

MY THOUGHTS:

Additional scriptures I studied:

Ideas for additional study:

Make a list of Korhior's arguments and tactics. You may want to even do a compare and contrast between his teachings to those of the other anti-Christs we have studied like Zeerom (Alma 10-11), Amlici (Alma 2), and Nehor (Alma 1). How are these same arguments and tactics (ie. "great swelling words" in Alma 28:31) still used today to deceive followers of Christ. After you make your list try to re-write some of his arguments in your own words or how they would sound today.

Why do you think Korihor's arguments appealed to so many women? How do his arguments still appeal to women? Do you think Satan targets women differently than he does men, if so how?

How does Alma respond to Korihor's arguments? What can you learn from his example about how to deal with anti- Mormon or anti-Christ messages?

CONVERTED ZORAMITE WOMEN

Scripture references:

Alma 35:14

What I know about them:

Words I looked up:

Questions I have about them:

MY THOUGHTS:

Additional scriptures I studied:

Ideas for additional study:

Make a story board of the Zoramites' story. It begins in Alma 31 and ends in Alma 35. What type of people are they? Who do they remind you of today? Why do some of the people listen and others do not? Where do they eventually end up?

In Alma 32 Alma gives a powerful sermon on faith. Use this chapter to do add to your topic study on faith that you began with the Wife of Queen Lamoni. It may help to draw pictures of what Alma describes. How do you think that this sermon would have affected the Zoramite women, especially Alma's teachings in Alma 32: 23?

What type of persecution have you faced for your faith or your beliefs? How much persecution do you think your testimony could withstand? How can these women's example help strengthen your dedication to your faith?

ISABEL

Scripture references:

Alma 39:3-4

What I know about her:

Words I looked up:

Questions I have about her:

MY THOUGHTS:

Additional scriptures I studied:

Ideas for additional study:

What do you think it means that she "did steal away the hearts of many" (Alma 39:3-4). What can that phrase teach us about the type of influence women have over men, for good or for evil?

The Hebrew form of the name Jezebel is Îzebel. The story of Jezebel is one that happened before Nephi and Lehi's time and so it likely that the Nephites were familiar with it. It is probable that Isabel's name was some form of this wicked Queen's name and that it may have been her real name or a name given to her because of her actions. Study the story of Jezebel in the Bible (1 Kings 16:31; 18:4-19; 19:1, 2; 21:5-25; 2 Kings 9). What attributes does she have that may have been similar to Isabel?

Study Alma's teachings to his son Corianton (Alma 39- 42) making note of what principles and doctrines Alma taught. What was it that Corianton did not understand about the gospel that led him to sin? What does Alma teach him that helps him understand? How can this pattern of teaching be helpful to you in your own life? How might you use it to teach youth?

IVES OF THE NEPHITES WHO DEFENDED THEIR FREEDOM

Scripture references:

Alma 43:9, 45, 46
Alma 44:5
Alma 46:12
Alma 48:10, 24
Alma 58:12

What I know about them:

Words I looked up:

Questions I have about them:

MY THOUGHTS:

Additional scriptures I studied:

Ideas for additional study:

Make a timeline of the war chapters in Alma 43- 62, you may need to tape several of them together to make it long enough. Make special note on your timeline of the times women are mentioned and events you feel would have specifically affected them.

In Alma 44: 5 Moroni states that they owe their wives and their children "sacred support." Ponder on this phrase. What do you think Moroni meant? How do men, in their roles of defending and providing for women and children offer "sacred support"? How have you seen or felt this type of support (or lack of support) in your life?

In Alma 50: 23 it states that "there never was a happier time among the people of Nephi". Why do you think the people were happy even amongst wars and contentions? What can their example teach you about happiness and trials?

LAMANITE QUEEN WHO MARRIED AMALICKIAH

Scripture references:

Alma 47:32-35
Alma 52:12

What I know about her:

Words I looked up:

Questions I have about her:

MY THOUGHTS:

Additional scriptures I studied:

Ideas for additional study:

What can this woman teach you about the role of Queens among the Lamanites? What type of position and power did this woman have?

Step into her shoes for a moment and try to imagine what she may have felt after her husband's death. What did she do? What was she afraid of? How do you think her fears influenced her choices? What would you have done similar or differently?

Why do you think this woman was deceived by Amalickiah? What were the consequences of her choice to marry him, for her and for her people? How might this story be used to teach young women about dating and choosing a good marriage companion?

MORIANTON'S MAID SERVANT

Scripture references:

Alma 50:30-31

What I know about her:

Words I looked up:

Questions I have about her:

MY THOUGHTS:

Additional scriptures I studied:

Ideas for additional study:

Her story is a powerful example of how important women's voices and women's experiences are. How did her courage to share her story and to speak against things that were wrong influence her people and Moroni's people? What do you think would have happened if she hadn't been brave enough to leave and to share her story?

This woman had been abused but she was not afraid to flee from her abuser and to testify against him. How might her story be empowering for women who have experienced abuse? How can sharing and speaking about their experiences help them, as well as others?

Consider taking some time to write in your journal, create art work, or in some other way express a part of your personal story that you feel hesitant or scared to share with others. Is there something that you have been ashamed of that you don't need to be? How could sharing your story benefit you and others?

WOMEN OF THE CITY BOUNTIFUL

Scripture references:

Alma 53:7

What I know about them:

Words I looked up:

Questions I have about them:

MY THOUGHTS:

Additional scriptures I studied:

Ideas for additional study:

What important insight does this verse give us into what the women and children experienced while the men were fighting wars? Make a list of trials these women were facing and what type of relief they needed. What other types of burdens do you think these women shouldered? How can this knowledge help you "see" and appreciate what the women experienced during the wars of the Book of Mormon?

How can you relate to these women? Have there been times when the men in your life have been absent or too busy to help you? How have you coped in such situations? What can this story teach you about how God feels about women and children?

Bountiful became a stronghold for holding Lamanite prisoners and a place for "preparing for war… and in making fortifications" (Alma 53:7). What role do you think these women played in those preparations? You may want to draw pictures of what these fortifications looked like (see Alma 50: 1-12; 53: 3-5) . What spiritual lessons can we learn from Moroni's example of taking time to prepare and fortify?

Scripture references:

Alma 54:3, 11-12
Alma 55:17-24
Alma 58:30-31
Alma 60:17

What I know about them:

Words I looked up:

Questions I have about them:

MY THOUGHTS:

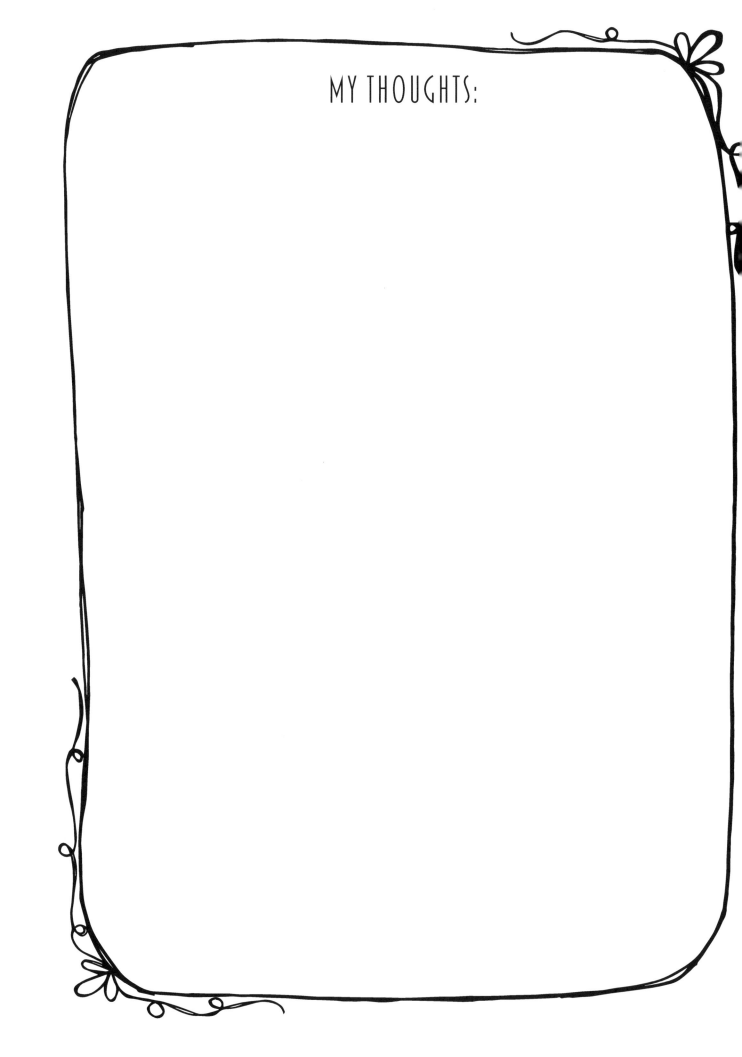

Additional scriptures I studied:

Ideas for additional study:

Draw a storyboard of the events in Alma 55. What stands out to you in this story? What roles would the women have had ?

How long do you think these women would have been prisoners? What do you imagine their living conditions were? Imagine how you would feel to be taken prisoner along with all (or part of) your children? Why do you think the Nephites did not take women or children prisoner?

How did Moroni keep the promise he made to Amalickiah that if he would not free a man and his wife and his children that he would "come against you... yea, even I will arm my women and my children." (Alma 54: 12)

What do you think happens to the women and children mentioned in Alma 58: 30-31?

WIVES AND CHILDREN OF THE 10,000 NEPHITE SOLDIERS AT THE CITY OF JUDEA

Scripture references:

Alma 56:28

What I know about them:

Words I looked up:

Questions I have about them:

MY THOUGHTS:

Additional scriptures I studied:

Ideas for additional study:

It is important to remember that in almost all wars throughout history women have traveled with armies, as cooks, nurses, and companions. These verse tell us that the Nephite and Lamanite armies were no different, and that along with the soldiers stationed in Judea there were also wives and children. How does it change your perspective of the war stories in Alma to know that there would have been women, Nephite and Lamanite, accompanying all of the military campaigns and conflicts?

We often hear about the mothers of the stripling warriors (see Alma 56:47-48; 57:21), but don't often talk about their fathers. Alma 56: 27-28 gives us a beautiful glimpse into how they supported their sons. What can you learn from their example? How was their involvement in their son's lives different than their mothers? How did these mothers and fathers work together?

How much food do you think it would take to support 10,000 men as well as their wives and children? What role do you imagine that women had in growing the food and making clothing to support these Nephite armies?

MOTHERS OF THE 2,060 STRIPLING WARRIORS

Scripture references:

Alma 56:47-48
Alma 57:21

What I know about them:

Words I looked up:

Questions I have about them:

MY THOUGHTS:

Additional scriptures I studied:

Ideas for additional study:

Use the dates in the bottom right corner of your Book of Mormon to figure out (approximately) how many years passed between the time that the Anti-Nephi-Lehi's were converted (Alma 23) and the time of the stripling warriors (Alma 56-57). How old do you think their mothers would have been? What would these women have experienced?

In describing the faith of the Anti-Nephi-Lehi's Mormon says that they, "never did look upon death with any degree of terror, for their hope and views of Christ and the resurrection, therefore death was swallowed up to them by the victory of Christ over it." (Alma 27:28). How do you think these women's understanding of the atonement influenced their son's lives and faith? In the Index use the scriptures listed under "Jesus Christ, Atonement Through" (page 176) and "Jesus Christ, Resurrection of" (page 182) to make a list (or scatter chart) of doctrines and principles about the atonement and resurrection. What did these women understand about the atonement and resurrection that made them fearless? How can you gain that same type of knowledge?

What type of covenants had these women made (see Alma 24)? What can their story teach you about the power of making and keeping covenants to God? How does keeping your covenants bless the lives of your posterity?

NEPHITE WOMEN AND CHILDREN WHO MIGRATED NORTHWARD

Scripture references:

Alma 63: 4-10

What I know about them:

Words I looked up:

Questions I have about them:

MY THOUGHTS:

Additional scriptures I studied:

Ideas for additional study:

Draw pictures of the different groups that migrated northward. How did they all travel? What was different about them? What was the same? Why do you think that there were so many people who migrated at this time?

Think of a time when you have moved from your home. What motivated you? What challenges did you face? What blessings did you gain from your move? How might these women's experiences been similar or different from yours?

Modern day prophets have repeatedly declared that Polynesians are Lamanites, and there is a strong tradition among Latter-day Saints connecting the people who sailed in Hagoth's ships with the Polynesians. If you are interested in learning more about this idea there is a good article by Robert E. Parsons entitled, "Hagoth and the Polynesians," that can be found online or in The Book of Mormon: Alma, the Testimony of the Word, ed. Monte S. Nyman and Charles D. Tate Jr. (Provo, UT: Religious Studies Center, Brigham Young University, 1992), 249–62.

Scripture references:

Helaman 1:27

What I know about them:

Words I looked up:

Questions I have about them:

MY THOUGHTS:

Additional scriptures I studied:

Ideas for additional study:

How many cities did Coriantumr take? How many women and children do you think his actions would have affected? What would these women have experienced?

Read 3 Nephi 11:29-30 about contention. As you study Helaman 1 look for ways in which contention leads to violence and destruction. What things in your life cause contention or make you feel contentious? What can you do to minimize the contention in your life?

The Nephites focused on protecting their outer cities but failed to fortify their inner cities. Coriantumr saw this and went straight for where they were the weakest, in the center. What spiritual application can you take from this story? How might it help you fortify the parts of your spirit and testimony that are weak?

WOMEN WHO TOILED AND SPUN ALL MANNER OF CLOTH

Scripture references:

Helaman 6:13
Mosiah 10:5
(indirectly Ether
10:24)

What I know about them:

Words I looked up:

Questions I have about them:

MY THOUGHTS:

Additional scriptures I studied:

Ideas for additional study:

"Fine-twined linen" is a phrase that is used often throughout the scriptures. Use the "search" function in the online scriptures (scriptures.lds.org) and type in the phrase "fine twined linen". Take time to study these scriptures and make a list of all the items that were made from "fine twined linen." What do many of these object have in common? How might this type of cloth have been associated with the temple that we know the Nephites built (see 2 Nephi 5:16). You may also want to do the same type of search with the phrase "clothe nakedness".

Do a compare and contrast between these two (or all three) scriptures where women are described as weaving and making cloth. What do you notice is similar about all three situations, what do you notice is different about them?

Why do you think Mormon mention women's production of cloth in his list of the people's riches? What can it tell you about the role women played in Book of Mormon life and society?

In ancient times Goddesses were often portrayed as spinning and weaving. How might the work women did to make cloth in order "to clothe our nakedness" be a spiritual endeavor? In what ways do women still work to clothe their families and their communities?

Scripture references:

Helaman 11:33

What I know about them:

Words I looked up:

Questions I have about them:

MY THOUGHTS:

Additional scriptures I studied:

Ideas for additional study:

Use the Pride Cycle sheet in the appendix to map out the cycle or pride in Helaman 11. How do you think this cycle of pride may have contributed to these women's abductions? What effect did their abductions have on the Nephites?

Use the Pride cycle sheet in the appendix to map out your own personal pride cycle. Where have you been, where are you at now, and where are you going? What can you do to break the cycle and stay humble.

What do you think happened to these women? Why do you think we don't ever hear about them again?

In Helaman 15:2 Samuel the Lamanite makes a prophecy about the plight of the Nephite women if they don't repent. What do you find interesting or upsetting about this prophecy? What do you think it means that "your houses shall be left desolate" (Helaman 15:1)? How does that apply to women?

LAMANITE WOMEN WHO UNITED WITH THE NEPHITES

Scripture references:

3 Nephi: 2:12-16

What I know about them:

Words I looked up:

Questions I have about them:

MY THOUGHTS:

Additional scriptures I studied:

Ideas for additional study:

What do you think the difference was between the youth mentioned in 3 Nephi 2:16 and those described in 3 Nephi 1: 28-30? How can you help the youth in your life be strong and dedicated to the gospel?

In 3 Nephi 2: 15 it says that these Lamanites' "curse was taken from them, and their skin became white." It is worthwhile to note that in 1981 the First Presidency changed the wording in 2 Nephi 30:6 which says, "and many generations shall not pass away among them, save they shall be a white and delightsome people" to a "pure and delightsome people." This change can help us better understand what the words "white" and "curse" mean when they are used in the Book of Mormon. To do a deeper study of this topic look up the worlds "white" and "curse" in the Index and do a scatter chart. What do you notice about the reasons that people are "cursed" by the Lord? What do those who have their "curse" removed or who become "white" have in common? Why do you think the Nephites used skin color to describe this change in people?

WOMEN UNITED AGAINST THE GADIANTON ROBBERS

Scripture references:

3 Nephi: 3:13

What I know about them:

Words I looked up:

Questions I have about them:

MY THOUGHTS:

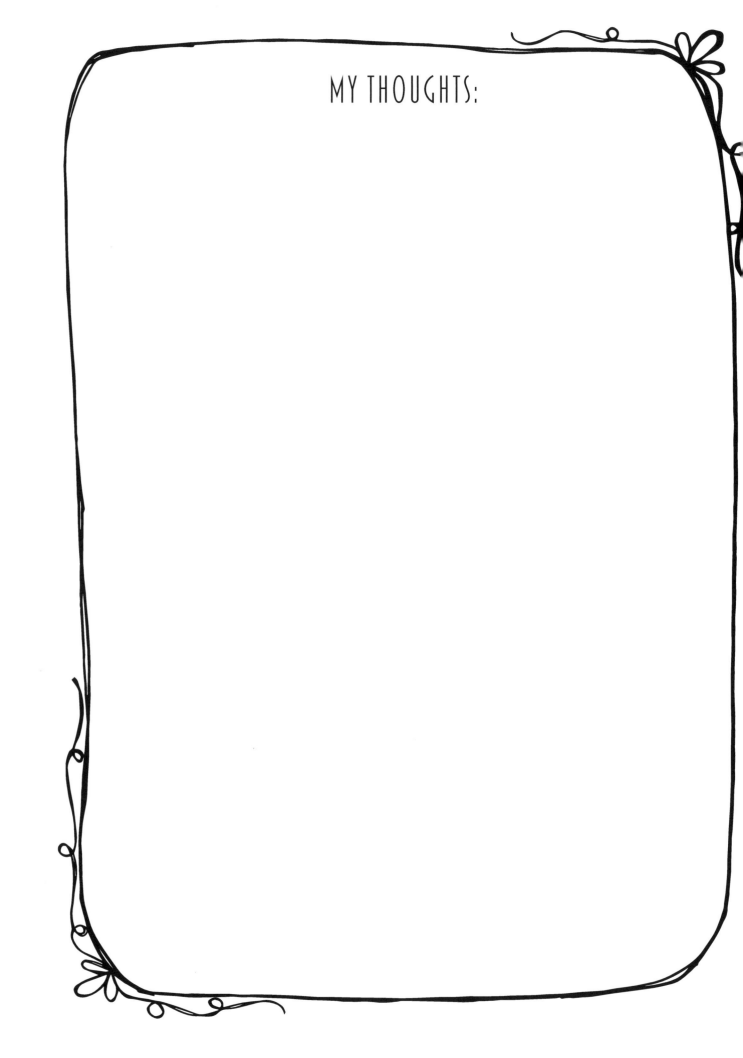

Additional scriptures I studied:

Ideas for additional study:

Use your Index to look up the topic "Gadianton Robber" and make a timeline of when and how this group started and what their actions were. As you study make a list (or a character sketch) of the characteristics of the Gadianton Robbers. Is there a group of people today who remind you of Gadianton robbers? What can you do to fortify and unite your family against such influences?

As you study 3 Nephi 3-5 make a list of all the things that the people did to defeat the Gadianton robbers. Which things do you think were the most important things they did, why? How did they finally put an end to the secret combinations, at least for awhile (see 3 Nephi 5:1-7)?

What can this story teach you about the importance of being unified? How might this story be applied to your church family as well as your personal family?

WOMEN KILLED DURING THE DESTRUCTION

Scripture references:

3 Nephi 8:25
3 Nephi 9:2

What I know about them:

Words I looked up:

Questions I have about them:

MY THOUGHTS:

Additional scriptures I studied:

Ideas for additional study:

3 Nephi 8:25 makes specific mention of the "mothers and our fair daughters, and our children" who were killed in the city of Moronihah. It appears that this was a large city that was completely destroyed. To learn more about what happened to the women in Moronihah see 3 Nephi 8:10; 9: 5.

What reasons does Christ's give for why some people were destroyed and others weren't (see 3 Nephi 9: 2-13)? How do we often bring our own trials or sorrows upon ourselves?

Think of a time when you have been in a natural disaster or another scary situation. How did you react? Was it how you expected? How do you think these people reacted to such huge and widespread calamities? What do you think they would have felt?

WOMEN AND GIRLS PRESENT AT JESUS'S APPEARANCE

Scripture references:

3 Nephi 17: 1-25
3 Nephi 18:21; 19:1

What I know about them:

Words I looked up:

Questions I have about them:

MY THOUGHTS:

Additional scriptures I studied:

Ideas for additional study:

Make a timeline or a storyboard of the experiences these women would have had, beginning in 3 Nephi 8. Which experiences do you think would have affected you the most powerfully? How might these experiences have been different for women than for men?

Think of a girl in your life whom you love. Can you imagine what it would feel like to see her encircled by angels in the midst of fire (3 Nephi 17:24)? Take a moment and draw a picture of what that might look or feel like. What do you hope this girl would understand or feel? How can you help her feel those things by being a ministering angel in her life?

Christ commanded the people to "go ye unto your homes and ponder upon the things which I have said" (see 3 Nephi 17:3) so that they would be able to understand what He had taught them, and be ready to learn more. In 3 Nephi 19 we read about what he taught them and what they received. How do you think taking the time to ponder and reflect on what they had learned helped them to be ready to receive more? How might you apply this same pattern in your life?

NEPHITE WOMEN AT THE TIME OF MORMON

Scripture references:

Mormon 2:23
Mormon 6:7, 19
Mormon 8:40

What I know about them:

Words I looked up:

Questions I have about them:

MY THOUGHTS:

Additional scriptures I studied:

Ideas for additional study:

As you read Mormon 2-5 make a list of words and phrases that describe the Nephites at this point in the Book of Mormon. What do you notice? How have the people changed from the previous chapters? How many years have passed since the time that Jesus visited the Americas? (see Mormon 8:6)

Make a timeline of the events leading up to the destruction of the Nephites. Start in Mormon 1 and end in Mormon 8. Make note of how many times Mormon leads his people into battle, and how his attitude changes each time. What is it that leads the Nephites to destruction? How might we be in danger of making some of the same mistakes that the Nephites made?

Mormon 6: 16-7 and Mormon 7 contain the words that Mormon wished that his people would have understood before they were destroyed. Read his words and then imagine that you could write a letter to your posterity (your children, grandchildren or great grandchildren). What would you say to them? What would you want them to know? Take time to pray to know what the Lord would have you say and then write that letter in your journal or in another special place.

WOMEN OFFERED AS SACRIFICES BY THE LAMANITES

Scripture references:

Mormon 4: 14-15, 21

What I know about them:

Words I looked up:

Questions I have about them:

MY THOUGHTS:

Additional scriptures I studied:

Ideas for additional study:

These women lived in the city of Teancum. As you study Mormon 4 think about the events that surround the battle of Teancum and what it would have been like to have been a Nephite woman in that city. How long did the battle go on?

What do you think it means that "every heart was hardened"? How do you think this resulted in violence? Can you think of times when you have seen people harden their hearts? What does it look or feel like when someone hardens their heart?

We know that the Incas and the Mayans, who were decedents of the Lamanties, commonly practiced human sacrifice. Study the entry for "sacrifice" in the Bible Dictionary (pages 765-767). In what ways do you think that human sacrifice was a corruption of the Mosaic law (which the Nephites also would have practiced) and Christ's atonement?

The story of Abraham in The Pearl of Great Price gives a very descriptive account of a human sacrifice, which may have been similar to what the Lamanites were practicing (see Abraham 1:7-15, and Facsimile No.1). In addition there are several other accounts of human sacrifice in the Bible as well. Study these accounts and notice what is similar and different about them. (See Judges 11:30-40; 1 Samuel 15:33; Jeremiah 7:31-32; 32:35; 1 Kings 16:34; 2 Kings 3:2-27; 2 Kings 23:10; 2 Chronicles 33:6; Ezekiel 16:20; 20:31; Joshua 6:26.)

WOMEN WHO TRAVELED WITH THE BROTHER OF JARED

Scripture references:

Ether 1:33, 37, 41
Ether 2:1
Ether 6:3

What I know about them:

Words I looked up:

Questions I have about them:

MY THOUGHTS:

Additional scriptures I studied:

Ideas for additional study:

Study the story of Jared and his brother beginning in Ether 1: 33- Ether 3 and Ether 6. Draw a timeline or a storyboard of the events. How do you think that women would have factored into this story? What would they have experienced and how might their experiences have been different from the men's?

Read Genesis 11, which is the same time period as Jared and his family. What do you think it means that the Lord "confounded" the people's language (if you have no idea look "confounded" up in the dictionary or thesaurus)? Why do you think Jared and his family were so concerned that it not happen to them? What were they willing to sacrifice in order to make sure that their language was preserved?

In the Book of Ether we get the genealogy of the Jaredites, which is unique because it lists how daughters each man had. Read through the verses and figure out how many daughters each person had, it might require a bit of math in some cases. You may also want to make note of any additional details given about them or who their brothers, fathers, and grandfathers were: The brother of Jared (Ether 6:15-18, 20), The friends of Jared (Ether 6:16-18), Jared (Ether 6:20), Orihah (Ether 7:1) , Corihor (Ether: 7:4, 14), Shule (Ether 7:12, 26)

WICKED DAUGHTER OF JARED

Scripture references:

Ether 8:8-12, 17
Ether 9:4

What I know about her:

Words I looked up:

Questions I have about her:

MY THOUGHTS:

Additional scriptures I studied:

Ideas for additional study:

It is important to note that she wasn't the daughter of Jared who came over on the barges, but rather a later Jared (Ether 8:1-7). What was her father like and how do you think his influence in her life shaped who she was and what she did?

Do a character sketch for her. How does she differ from the righteous women you have already studied? Also, notice that in Ether 8:8-9 the word "exceedingly" is used twice to describe her. How might these two characteristics have been a bad combination?

The ancient oaths that the Daughter of Jared was referring to are mentioned more in Moses 5: 16- 33 in the story of Cain. Do a compare and contrast between the story of Cain in Moses 5 and the story of Akish in Ether 8: 13-26. Additionally, Moroni mentions in Ether 8: 20 &24 that these oaths and combinations "are had among all people" and that it "bringeth to pass the destruction of all people." How do you see these same type of mindsets and actions being played out in our world today? What can you do to combat them?

Ether 8: 17 says that it was "the daughter of Jared who put it into his [Jared's] heart to search up these things of old." How might you use her story to teach young women about the type of power and influence they have over others, especially men? How did the daughter of Jared misuse her power?

DAUGHTERS OF OMER

Scripture references:

Ether 8:4
Ether 9: 2-3

What I know about them:

Words I looked up:

Questions I have about them:

MY THOUGHTS:

Additional scriptures I studied:

Ideas for additional study:

What had these women experienced (Ether 8: 1-7)? Who were their brothers? What eventually happens to them? Do their experiences remind you of any other stories in the Book of Mormon? Why do you think that the Lord often directs righteous people to flee and to go into the wilderness?

How did these women differ from the Daughter of Jared (see Ether 8)? What good choices did they make that possitively affected them, their family and their people? On the other hand what were the consequences of the daughter of Jared's choices for her, for her family and for her people (see Ether 9: 4-12)?

What can these women and the daughter of Jared teach us about the importance of father-daughter relationships? How can fathers teach and nurture their daughters and how can daughters support and honor their fathers?

Even though we don't know exactly where events in the Book of Mormon took place we do have a good guess at where Cummorah, the place where the Nephites were destroyed, is because of the Hill Cummorah where Joseph Smith found the gold plates. Based on the description of their journey in Ether 9: 3 where do you imagine these women living and how might that make them more "real" to you?

WO WIVES OF CORIANTUM

Scripture references:

Ether 9:24

What I know about them:

Words I looked up:

Questions I have about them:

MY THOUGHTS:

Additional scriptures I studied:

Ideas for additional study:

Draw pictures of these two women and then make a list of how they were similar and how they were different. What unique challenges would each have faced? What blessings would each have experienced? How do you imagine they were a support to Coriantum?

What type of man was Coriantum and his father Emer (see Ether 9: 14-23)? Fill out a pride cycle sheet for the generations listed starting with Emer (Ether 9:14) and ending with his great-grandson Heth (Ether 9:25-35). How many years did it take for them to go through the pride cycle?

Can you imagine living to be 102 years old like Corinatum's first wife? If you were to live to be that old what do you hope you would have accomplished in your life? Take the time to write down some of the goals you have for your future. What things are most important to you? Are you living your life in a way that those goals will be accomplished?

WOMEN OF ETHER 10

Scripture references:

Ether 10

What I know about them:

Words I looked up:

Questions I have about them:

MY THOUGHTS:

Additional scriptures I studied:

Ideas for additional study:

Ether 10 gives a genealogy of the Jaredite kings and their families. Make a timeline or a list of all the kings starting with Heth (Ether 9: 25- Ether 10: 1) and ending with Com (Ether 10:34). As you record each king make a note of the women mentioned (usually in the form of "he begat sons and daughters") and if the king was righteous or not. Using a different color pencil to mark for wicked and righteous kings may help you to see the ups and downs of the Jaredites easier.

There is more information given about Lib and his people than any of the other kings in Ether 10. What was the world of the Jaredites like under his reign? Why do you think that there "could never be a people more blessed than were they" (Ether 10: 28)?

AIR DAUGHTERS AND WOMEN OF THE PEOPLE OF CORINATUMR

Scripture references:

Ether 13:17-22
Ether 14:2, 17, 22, 31
Ether 15:2, 12-25

What I know about them:

Words I looked up:

Questions I have about them:

MY THOUGHTS:

Additional scriptures I studied:

Ideas for additional study:

These women saw the destruction of the Jaredite people. Yet they were given plenty of warning by Ether and other prophets. Go back and study the prophecies of Ether (Ether 12 &13) and make three lists: what he teaches them, what he warns them about, and what they needed to do not to be destroyed. It is also interesting to note that Moroni (who had also just witnessed the destruction of his people) inserts his own insights and prophecies in among Ether's words. How might the words of these two prophets be important for our day?

Why do you think the sons and daughters of Coriantumr, Corihor, and Com are called "fair"? How might this relate to what Mormon says about his people in Mormon 6:19?

Millions of women and children were killed in the battle between Coriantumr and Shiz (see Ether 15:2). As you study Ether 14 and 15 create a mental imagine your mind (or draw a story board) of what these women would have witnessed and experienced. Can you think of any groups of people (current or historical) who have experienced similar amounts of violence? What type of desperation would it take for a people to arm even their women and even their children (see Ether 15: 15)?

NEPHITE WOMEN IN SHERRIZAH

Scripture references:

Moroni 9: 7-8, 16-19

What I know about them:

Words I looked up:

Questions I have about them:

MY THOUGHTS:

Additional scriptures I studied:

Ideas for additional study:

There are three different groups of Nephite women that Mormon mentions to his son Nephi in these verses: 1) women taken prisoner by the Lamanites (Moroni 9:7), 2) widows, daughters, and old women left in Sherrizah (Moroni 9:16) , and 3) women who fled to the army of Aaron (Moroni 9: 17, see footnote "a"). Draw a picture of each group of women and make a list of what their experiences were, what their challenges would have been, and how Mormon felt about them.

Mormon 9 is a letter that Mormon sent to his son Moroni during the wars that were taking place in Mormon 2- 4. After reading Moroni 9 go back and read Mormon 2- 4 noticing what the Nephites were experiencing and how these women's experiences would have fit in with these events. How is their situation similar to that of the Jaredites you recently studied in Ether 14 and 15?

In Moroni 9: 19 Mormon says, "the suffering of our women and children… doth exceed everything." Yet then in Moroni 9: 25 he tells his son "may not the things which I have written grieve thee, to weigh thee unto death, but may Christ lift thee up." How can our knowledge and faith in Christ help us face the wickedness and extreme trials of this life? How has Christ lifted you up in times of great darkness and despair?

DAUGHTERS OF THE LAMANITES HELD PRISONER IN MORIANTUM

Scripture references:

Moroni 9:9-10

What I know about them:

Words I looked up:

Questions I have about them:

MY THOUGHTS:

Additional scriptures I studied:

Ideas for additional study:

After having just studied what the Nephite women suffered at the hands of the Lamanties (Moroni 9: 7-8, 16-19) whose actions do you think were worse—the Nephite men or the Lamanite men? Why?

As you study Moroni 9 make a list of the attributes exhibited by the Nephite men. How do you think that these attributes led to abuse and violence against women? How might we use this example to help teach our young men about what it means to be a man of God and how to treat women?

It is interesting to remember that the book of Moroni are "extras" that Moroni added in because as he said, "I have not yet as perished" (Moroni 1:1) and which he hoped would, "be of worth unto my brethren the Lamanties, in some future day" (Moroni 1:4). Why do you think that Moroni chose to include this letter at the very end of the Book of Mormon? How might it tie in with his closing words in Moroni 10?

APPENDIX

STORY BOARD FOR:

TIME LINE

CHARACTER STUDY

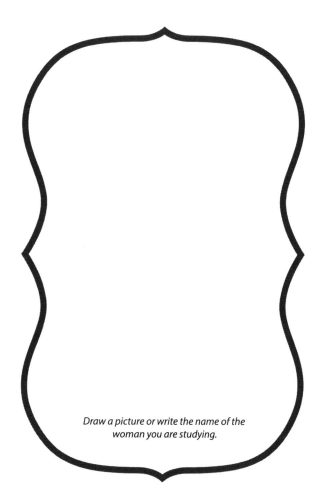

Draw a picture or write the name of the
woman you are studying.

COMPARE AND CONTRAST

COMPARE AND CONTRAST

COMPARE AND CONTRAST

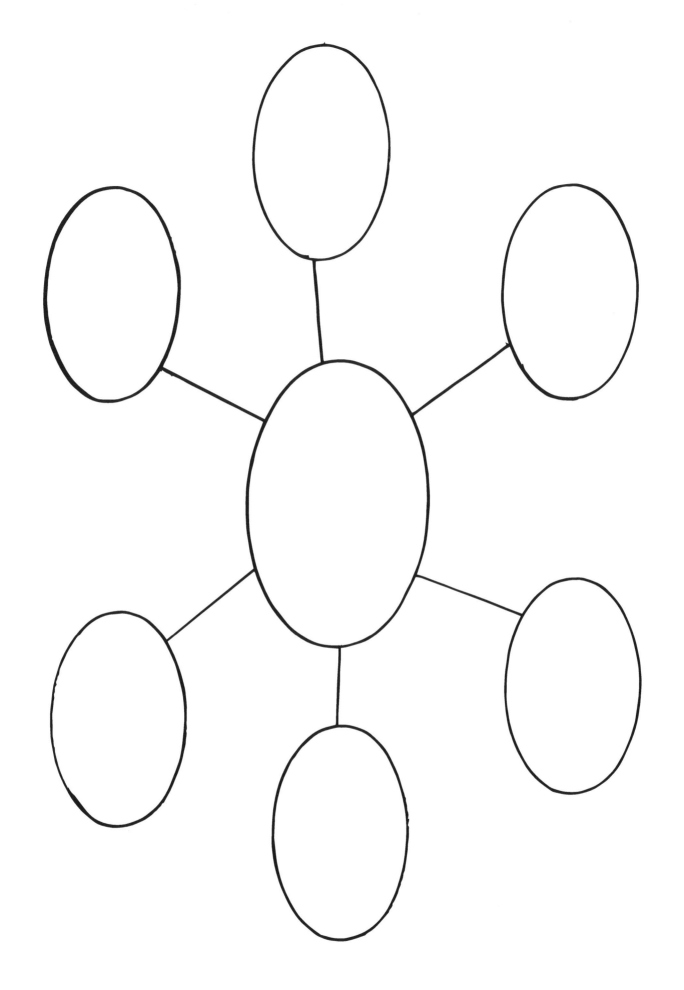

SCATTER CHART

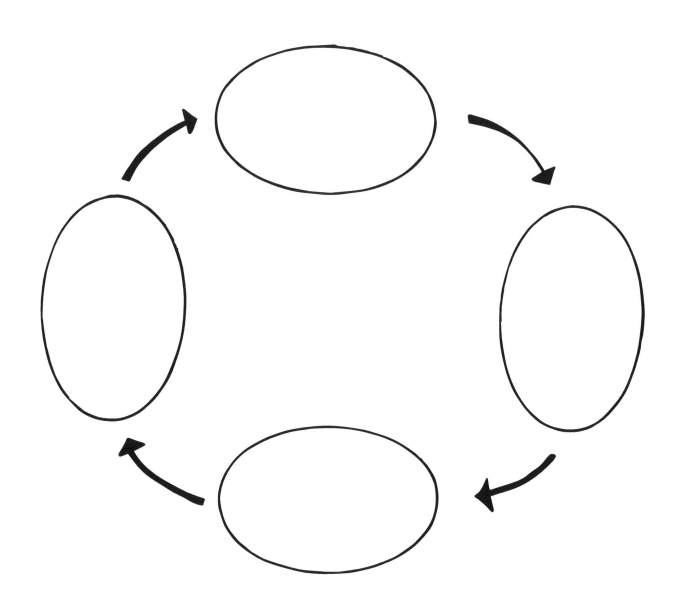

PRIDE CYCLE

Scripture references:

What I know about her:

Words I looked up:

Questions I have about her:

MY THOUGHTS:

Additional scriptures I studied:

Ideas for additional study: